Bedtime History

25 Inspirational Stories for Kids

Breck LeSueur

Bedtime History

Ordering Information:
Quantity sales. Special discounts are available on quantity purchases by corporations, associations, and others at www.lulu.com.

Printed in the United States of America

Neil Armstrong
First to the Moon

Tegla Laroupe
Marathon Hero

Sir Edmund Hillary
Knight of Mount Everest

Gail Halvorsen
The Berlin Candy Bomber

Bob Feller
The Heater from Van Meter

Joan of Arc
Heroine of Hope

The Chunnel
World's Longest Undersea Tunnel

Rosetta Space Probe
Comet Exploration Mission

Newsies
The Newsboys Strike of 1899

Stars
A History

George Lucas
The Making of Star Wars

Nancy Wake
World War Commando

Nelly Blye
Around the World in 72 Days

Mahatma Ghandi
Faithful Leader of Peace

Sacajawea
Noble Explorer

Abraham Lincoln
From a Log Cabin to Defender of the Union

The Navy SEALs
America's Elite Fighting Force

Sylvester Stallone
The Rocky Story

Kerri Strugg
Olympic Gymnast

Benjamin Franklin
The First American

"Buffalo Bill" Cody
Greatest Showman of the West

J.K. Rowling
The Harry Potter Story

The Pony Express
Brave Riders of the American West

Sandra Porter
My Grandmother

Neil Armstrong

First to the Moon

Neil Armstrong was born in Ohio and was the oldest brother in his family. When he was little his father took him to a show where airplanes flew and raced across the sky. From the moment he saw airplanes he loved them. He wanted to fly airplanes himself. He wanted to become a pilot. Not long after he saw his first airplanes, Neil got to fly in an airplane. After this he knew for sure he wanted to be a pilot. When Neil was fourteen he took his first flying lessons. By the time he was sixteen he had a pilot's license, which meant he could fly a plane all by himself.

Neil loved to fly planes, but he also loved to learn about them. He built his own small model planes and also did experiments on them to see which designs flew the best. He designed a wind tunnel in his house. A wind tunnel is a tunnel which forces wind through it so one can test model airplanes.

Neil loved airplanes but he also enjoyed learning about space. Often he would look up in the sky and wonder what was out among the stars and if people would ever go there. His neighbor had a big telescope that Neil often used to look at the planets and stars.

In school Neil listened to his teachers and did his homework, because he knew he would need to learn all he could in order to become a great pilot. When Neil got older he went to college and worked hard to learn about planes and engineering. Engineering is the science of building things, which for Neil was building airplanes.

While Neil was in college, a war started and he became a fighter pilot. His job was to fly airplanes off huge ships called aircraft carriers. He flew 78 missions during the war. One time his airplane was shot down and he had to eject out of the seat and parachute down to the ground. Fortunately, he was rescued and was safe.

After the war and after finishing college, Neil became a test pilot. A test pilot tries out new planes to make sure they are safe for others to fly and to help make them better. Sometimes it was a dangerous job, but Neil had courage and tested over 20 new planes. He even set a record for flying one of the fastest jets in the world.

Neil loved airplanes and space so he decided to become an astronaut, a pilot who flies to space! He had to work hard to become an astronaut, because only a few pilots get to become astronauts. While Neil was an astronaut the United States was planning its first space voyage to The Moon. Neil was picked to fly the space ship to the moon. While the ship was landing something wrong happened and Neil had to fly it down to the ground himself.

It was a scary situation, but Neil kept his cool and landed the spaceship safely. After the ship landed, Neil was the first person to step onto The Moon. People all over the world watched as Neil stepped onto The Moon and stuck an American flag there. Neil's footprint is still on The Moon today, because there is no wind there to blow it away.

Like Neil, you can be curious about the world around you. He was curious about airplanes and space and learned all he could about both of them so he could become an astronaut. He also listened closely in school and did his homework so he could become an airplane engineer. He was brave during the war when he was a fighter pilot. He was also brave when testing new airplanes. Before going to The Moon he had to practice day after day in order to pilot the first space craft. Like Neil, you can do great things when you are curious, brave, learn new things and practice, practice, practice!

Tegla Laroupe

Marathon Hero

This story begins in Africa in the small village of Kutomwony, Kenya. In the village lives a little girl named Tegla. Telga is very small for her age, but makes up for it with a big heart and a big smile. Life in Kutomwony isn't easy, most of the families are very poor and don't have electricity or water to use in their home. They work very hard and often have very little to eat.

Every morning Tegla wakes up very early and feeds her family's animals, and then makes breakfast for her brothers and sisters and helps dress them for the day. As soon as she's done with her chores she races out the door and out onto a dusty road.

Tegla goes to school like most children, but her school is six miles away, which is very, very far. She doesn't have a car or a bus, so she has to go there on foot. But Tegla doesn't just walk to school – she runs! In her bare feet! But Tegla loves running. At first she didn't love running to school. She only ran because she didn't want to be late. But the more she ran, the more she loved it. She could run the entire way without stopping once.

As Telga got older she wanted to run in a race, but others said, “you are too small, you are too weak. You should be taking care of your brothers and sisters, not running in races.” But Tegla didn’t listen to them. She started running races anyway. In fact, she was so good that she won a pair of shoes, so she didn’t have to run barefoot anymore!

Most of the people in Tegla’s village didn’t believe she could be a great racer, but she kept practicing anyway. She was persistent. Persistence is when you keep doing something, even when it is difficult or others don’t believe you can.

When Tegla got older she had the chance to go to the United States, to the big city of New York to run in a marathon. A marathon is a race that is 26 miles long. That is very, very, far! Before running the race others told her she was too small, that she wasn’t a good racer, that she should go back home. But Tegla said, “I will show you I am a good runner, I will win the race.” But no one believed such a small woman from a poor village in Africa could do such a big thing.

When the race began it didn’t seem like Tegla was doing very good. Many other runners were in front of her, it looked like she might lose. But she kept running, breathing deep, pushing ahead like she did when she was little and running to school in Africa. Toward the end of the race she began to run faster, and faster and faster. Soon she was passing everyone in front of her. The other racers didn't know how she was going so fast. Before long she was in front of every one else. No one believed it!

Everyone in the crowd started to cheer. Tegla dashed to the end. She had won the race! No woman from Africa had ever won the New York Marathon. Tegla had made history!

After winning the race Tegla was given thousands and thousands of dollars. She could have used the money to buy herself many nice things, she could have stayed in the nice city and never gone back to Africa. But Tegla remembered her little village, she remembered her family, and she remembered all the little boys and girls there who didn't get to go to school and did hard chores all day. She used her money to start a school for kids who wanted to run and used it to help other kids from Africa have a better chance in life. Tegla was kind and had charity. Charity is thinking about others and doing kind things to help them out.

Like Tegla, you can be active by running or playing sports or dancing or doing gymnastics. This helps your body grow strong and healthy. It also makes your mind strong. You can also be persistent — to keep trying and trying even when something seems very hard. It might be a homework problem or a chore, but like Tegla if you keep at it you can finish it. Like Tegla you can also be kind by using your time and other things you have to help others. Whenever someone else is in need you can remember Tegla and what she did to help make others happier.

Sir Edmund Hillary

The Knight of Mount Everest

Do you know the name of the tallest mountain in the world? It is called Mount Everest and it is 29,000 feet high. If you can imagine, it is the same as 1,000 houses stacked on top of each other. The little boy who grew up to be the man who climbed this mountain was named Sir Edmund Hillary.

Edmund was born in 1919 in the country of New Zealand. He was smaller than other kids his age and shy. Every day he got on a train and took it a very long way to school. On the train he liked to read books. His favorite books were about mountains and adventures. Little Edmund dreamed that one day he would go on his own adventures.

Edmund didn't stay small. When he was a teenager he grew very, very tall. By that time he didn't only dream about adventures, he started making his *own* adventures by climbing mountains. He loved climbing, especially in cold, snowy places. He had a passion for it. Passion is when you love doing something very much. Edmund practiced and practiced and became very good at climbing. He knew that all great adventurers have to practice and practice if they want to become very good at something. Edmund climbed over 34 mountains. That is a lot of practice!

Mount Everest is the highest mountain in the world in a country called Tibet. No one had ever climbed to the top. It was in a freezing cold place with fast wind and deep snow that made it very difficult and very dangerous to climb. All of the climbers in the world wanted to be the first person to make it to the top. Edmund wanted with all his heart to be the first one to the top.

When Edmund finally got the chance to try and reach the top of Mount Everest, he brought along a helper named Tenzing. Edmund and Tenzing had to wear warm clothes and carry heavy backpacks with all their food and other supplies. The mountain was very cold and much of the time they were hungry and tired, but Edmund and Tenzing kept going. They needed each other all along the way. They could not make it to the top alone. This is called teamwork. Teamwork is when people help each other to get something done.

When others turned around and went back down the mountain, Edmund remembered the adventures he read and dreamed about as a boy. Now *he* was the hero and this was *his* adventure.

Close to the top of Mount Everest there was a very high wall of ice that no else could climb. But Edmund was creative and strong and figured out a way to wriggle his way up a crack up into the top. The top of Mount Everest was so high that they could barely breath. It took them 20 days and they were only there for a few minutes, but they had reached their goal!

News about Edmund spread all around the world. When Edmund got home he met the Queen of England who made him a knight. In modern times a knight doesn't wear armor and ride a horse, instead they are someone who had done something great.

After Mount Everest, Edmund's adventures weren't over. He also went to the South Pole, then the North Pole, and wrote books about the amazing things he had done. Edmund became famous and made a lot of money from it. But Edmund didn't keep all the money for himself. He used the money to build schools, hospitals, churches and roads for villages in Tibet. When the newspapers wrote about Edmund and his adventures they said he was a hero, but he said he was just a normal person who had a big imagination, a lot of energy and worked very hard.

Like Edmund, you can read books and dream about doing great things. You can also have passion for things you enjoy. You can practice to get better at them. You can also use teamwork, which is working together to get things done, because you can't always do everything by yourself. Like Edmund, you can think about others who don't have all the nice things you have, and do what you can to help them out. And always remember, even mountains can be climbed if you work hard and take your goals one step at a time.

Gail Halvorsen

The Berlin Candy Bomber

Have you heard about World War 2? A world war is where many countries are fighting each other at the same time. The two groups fighting in World War 2 were called the Axis and the Allies. The Axis included Germany and Japan and Italy. The Allies included England, the United States, Russia and many other countries.

This story begins before World War 2 on a little farm in Utah in the United States. Living at this farm was a boy named Gail. Every day Gail helped his father grow sugar beets on the family farm. Gail's father taught him to work hard and to help others.

One day when Gail was working in the fields he heard a noise in the sky. He looked up and stared as planes flew over his head. From that moment he knew when he grew up he wanted to be a pilot.

When Gail was old enough, he joined the air force and learned how to fly. At this time a war was going on between England and Germany. Germany was trying to take over the other countries in Europe. Not long after Gail joined the air force Japanese airplanes attacked America's base at Pearl Harbor, Hawaii and America joined the Allies in the war. Gail's job was to fly bomber planes. A bomber's job is to drop bombs on the enemy.

World War 2 was long and hard and many soldiers were lost on both sides. War is a very sad time for the world and life is always better if peace can be made instead of war, but there are times when it becomes necessary to fight for freedoms. When the war was finally over instead of being harsh to Germany, America and the Allies decided to help its enemies in hopes that war would not happen again. The Allies helped Germany and Japan by giving them food and other supplies. Instead of bombing them now, Gail and the other pilots new job was to fly them the things they needed to survive. Gail was glad he could be helping instead of hurting the Germans now.

One day when Gail was in Germany, he was walking around and saw a bunch of kids crowded at a fence. They talked to him and thanked him for bringing them food. Gail had a strong feeling he should give them the gum he had in his pocket. The kids broke up the gum into little pieces and shared it with each other. They appreciated the gum. Appreciation is when you are thankful for something.

The next time Gail flew his plane over the crowd of kids, he thought about how much they enjoyed the candy and had a crazy idea about how he could give them more candy the next time. During the next trip Gail made little bags of candy and little parachutes for the bags. Then when he flew over the kids he threw the bags out the window. All of the bags of candy floated down to the ground. The kids picked up the candy and jumped for joy. Every time Gail flew over he wiggled his plane wings so the kids would know it was him. Soon the kids started calling him "Uncle Wiggly Wings."

Later other pilots learned about Gail throwing candy out of his plane, so they started doing the same thing. Newspapers all over the world started writing stories about what Gail and the other pilots were doing for the kids in Germany. Soon candy companies started sending candy to help in the effort. In America school children helped tie the candy into parachutes for Gail and the other pilots.

Even though the kids were happy to get the candy, what Gail really gave them was hope and that someone cared about them.

After making trips to Germany, Gail spent the rest of his life trying to help people in other ways. He is very old now but stills does what he can to make other people happy.

Many years later Gail met a man who said when he was a little boy living in Germany, he was walking to school one day. It was a rainy, cloudy day and he was very sad — then all of a sudden he saw a white parachute fall through the clouds and land right at his feet. He was so excited! He said he enjoyed eating the chocolate, but more importantly he knew that someone cared about him.

Like Gail, you can forgive your enemies. Forgiveness is when we are kind to someone even if they did something wrong to you. You can also be creative and think of fun ways to help others. You can help your family by cleaning your room or making your bed or helping your little brother or sister get dressed. You can make someone at school a nice card. You can be nice to someone at school who others aren't nice to. Like Gail, there is so much you can do to help others if you take the time to think about it.

Bob Feller

The Heater from Van Meter

This story is about a little boy named Bob Feller, who lived on a corn farm with his family in Iowa in the United States. Bob loved baseball and always looked forward to playing catch with his father after a long day of work. Bob practiced throwing a baseball everyday, but he always did his chores first. He always put his family and his work first because his father taught him the importance of hard work and priorities. Having priorities means doing important things first such as work and school before other things like fun and games. Bob's father saw how good he was becoming at baseball, so he decided to start growing wheat instead of corn because it would give them more time to practice together.

When Bob grew older he began playing baseball with a team in his town. An important man with a baseball team saw how fast Bob threw the ball, so he hired him to play for a major league team, the Cleveland Indians. Bob was only 17 years old when he pitched his first major league baseball game. He quickly became well known as one of fastest pitchers the league. His fastball was recorded at 104 to 107 miles per hour. That is very fast! Bob Feller also became the first pitcher to win 24 games before the age of 21.

Along with baseball, Bob had a great love for his country. After Japan attacked Pearl Harbor and the United States entered World War 2, Bob joined the United States Navy. The Navy said that Bob didn't need to go into battle and that he could stay where it was safe, but Bob said he wanted to be with the other soldiers where he could fight for his country. He was assigned to a battleship. When the war ended, Bob received many awards for his service.

After the war, Bob returned to playing with the Cleveland Indians and in 1948 they won World Series, which is the biggest championship in baseball. Bob was one of the greatest pitchers in baseball. He said that his skill and speed in pitching came from hard work milking cows, picking corn, and baling hay on his family farm. Even with all Bob's success in baseball, he always put important things before baseball, such as his family and his country.

Like Bob you can put important things first in your life, such as helping around the house, learning new things, and helping others. You can also practice at sports or other talents in order to become good like Bob. Practice is what you do to become better at something. Bob Feller showed us that even when someone becomes famous, they can still think about others by serving their country and doing good things.

Joan of Arc

Heroine of Hope

This story takes place in the Medieval Times, also called the Middle Ages. This was the time of kings and castles and knights and battles over kingdoms. It was also a time where many people had very little to eat and had to work very hard. In the country of France one of these poor families had a daughter named Joan. Joan worked every day to take care of the animals on their farm and sew and do other things to help the family survive. Young Joan was also very kind and always thinking about others. When others were sick she would visit them and bring them food to help them feel better. She was unselfish. Being unselfish is when you think about others rather than yourself.

At this time there was a war going on between Joan's country of France and another country, England, who controlled parts of France. From a young age Joan began to feel that her calling was to help the people of France be free again. She began to tell her family and other people in her village about her visions and strong beliefs. Soon other villages heard what Joan was saying about freedom and they believed her. Joan decided to journey to the king of France and tell him what she believed. At first the king didn't want to listen, but Joan was persistent. Persistence is when you keep doing something even when it is hard.

When the king finally listened to Joan's message of hope, he decided to let her go to battle. His servants dressed her in armor and put her on a horse and sent her off with the other soldiers. During the battle Joan carried a large flag. When the other soldiers saw Joan's flag it gave them hope, because they knew it was being carried by the brave young girl who believed France could again be free. Seeing Joan and her flag made them strong and they won battles whenever Joan was present. Joan was courageous and rode into battle even when it was dangerous. Courage is when you do something even though it may be scary.

During one particularly dangerous battle, Joan and the French soldiers had to ride boats past the enemy guns. The wind was weak that day so they were going very slow. The soldiers started to wonder if they would survive and began to panic. Joan stayed positive and spoke to them, encouraging them, reassuring them that it would be alright. Soon the winds picked up and they sailed past the enemy guns without getting hit.

Later during the battle the captains had attacked, but the army was not doing well. Joan heard what was happening and knew they needed her help. She jumped onto her horse and galloped to the front of the battle. There she saw many soldiers who were hurt. She had sympathy for them. Sympathy is when you feel bad for someone and want to help. Joan rode her horse into the battle and the soldiers began to cheer. They fought harder and eventually won the battle. Joan saw the enemy soldiers who had been hurt and tried to help them feel better, too. She didn't like seeing people hurt even though they were the enemy. Through many other battles Joan gave the French soldiers hope.

Eventually there was peace between France and England. Later Joan was captured and put in jail for a time, but no matter what happened to her, she stood up for her beliefs. There may be times in life that others will laugh at you or say mean things because of what you believe in, but like Joan you can ignore them and stand strong anyway. This is called having conviction.

Like Joan you can be unselfish by thinking about others instead of yourself. You can be brave and have courage when things are scary or hard. Next time you go to the doctor or take a test, think of how Joan went into battle and did hard things even when they weren't easy.

The Chunnel

World's Longest Undersea Tunnel

The Chunnel is the longest undersea tunnel in the world. This tunnel goes under the ground at the bottom of the ocean. England and France and separated by a large area of water called a "channel." Before the tunnel people had to take boats to go back and forth between the two countries. A long time ago someone had the idea to dig very deep below the ocean and all the way across to the other side.

Because it a tunnel and crosses a channel, it was called the "chunnel."

The first person who had the idea of digging this tunnel was a Frechman named Albert Mathieu. At the time they didn't have large digging machines, so they would have had to do much of it using shovels and horses and wagons. Later, others were going to try to dig the tunnel, at another time someone even started to dig from both sides, but France and England didn't get along so some were worried it would be used to attack each other. For this reason, they waited many years to start building the tunnel.

Finally, many years later, both England and France agreed on a plan and began digging from both sides. At that time they had better digging machines, so could work much faster. Even though the project was very difficult and took a lot of time, both sides kept working and working. It even cost much, much more than they expected, but they were determined to finish the tunnel to connect the two countries. They knew once the tunnel was finished it would make moving back and forth very fast and easy. It would also make both of the countries better friends because they could share more things very quickly. Along with digging the tunnel, they began to build train tracks, so a fast moving train could drive between England and French. Engineers had to be very smart and understand everything about the ground and ocean in order to build it. An engineer is someone who goes to school to learn how to build things.

After six years of digging and building, the chunnel was almost complete. Two workers, Graham Fagg and Phillipe Cozette, were chosen to break through the last wall of dirt that connected the two sides. Many reporters were there as well, since everyone in the world was watching them finish the tunnel. When Graham and Phillipe finished digging through, everyone cheered and gave hugs and celebrated. They were so excited to have the tunnel finally finished. Even today sometimes Graham and Phillipe call each other to remember what an exciting day it was when they helped finish the tunnel.

Soon afterward, the Queen of England, Queen Elizabeth, and the President of France, Francois Mitterand, took trains from both sides and met in the middle to shake hands and congratulate each other on the great achievement.

In the end, digging The Chunnel cost 16 billion dollars and even the lives of a few of the workers, but it was an amazing accomplishment. At its lowest point it is 250 feet deep. That is the same as 20 houses stacked on top of each other. It is 23 miles long and every day carries people and food and other things back and forth between France and England.

Like the engineers who built The Chunnel, you can learn math and science and other subjects that are in important. They had to read and study and finish tests the best they could in order to have the knowledge to build The Chunnel. You can also learn to work hard like the many workers who helped dig the tunnel and kept going and going even when it was difficult. Always remember great accomplishments take time, patience, practice and hard work.

Rosetta Space Probe

The First Comet Mission

Have you ever heard of a comet? A comet is a gigantic piece of ice, rock and dirt that flies through outer space at incredible speeds. Many comets are the size of mountains and when they journey through space have tails of gasses hundreds of thousands of meters long.

For a long time humans have seen comets in the sky and wondered about them. Some very smart scientists decided they wanted to learn more about comets so they decided to create a spaceship that would find a comet and land on it! This had never been done before, but they knew if they designed the spaceship right and worked out all of the math correctly they could make the landing happen.

Many different countries in Europe designed and started working on the spacecraft they would call “Rosetta.” It took many different engineers and scientists studying space and spaceships to know how Rosetta should work. Astronomers had to watch the comet flying through space and use advanced math to figure out how fast Rosetta needed to go in order to land on it.

When Rosetta was ready the engineers blasted the ship into outer space and the astronomers instructions gave it directions to fly. No humans were actually on board the Rosetta space probe, because it would be gone for a very long time and might be a very dangerous mission. The pilots flew the Rosetta sort of like you might fly a remote controlled car.

For *10 years* Rosetta flew through outer space. During this time it passed planets like Mars and asteroids, other rocks in space, and many places a space probe had never been. After 10 years Rosetta was finally close enough to the icy comet speeding through space. All of the engineers and scientists at mission control were very nervous. They had worked very hard for this day and had been very patient, waiting 10 years until they could land their ship. When the day finally came they watched in anticipation as Rosetta came into orbit of the gigantic comet. This particular comet was as big as a mountain.

Attached to Rosetta was a robot that would land on the comet and do experiments to learn more about the comet. When the time was right the lander shot out of Rosetta and raced toward the massive comet below. For a moment it seemed as thought it wouldn't work, the lander was off track. Then suddenly the lander shot spears out of its side and slammed into the ground of the comets. It used these hooks and ropes to pull itself down to the ground. When it hit the ground it tumbled and was broken in some places but eventually came to rest. Everyone at mission control cheered. The robot had landed, Rosetta space probe had completed its mission. This was the first time a robot had ever landed on a comet flying through space! The mission was a great success!

Once the lander, which they had called Phillae, had time to recharge its batteries it was able to do a few experiments and send the data back to earth. Because of Phillae, anstronomers learned about the water on comets and some of their metals.

Like the scientists and engineers who designed and built Rosetta, you should learn all you can about science and other subjects. They had to listen closely and study and do their homework to become skilled at what they do.

Astronomers also helped by learning about the stars. You can go out at night, look at the stars and watch shows and read about all of the amazing things happening in the sky above you. Waiting for Rosetta to finally reach the comment also took patience. They had to wait many years until it arrived. Over 2000 people worked on this project. This shows that teamwork is crucial to make great things happen.

Newsies

The Newsboys Strike of 1899

In 1899 many new people were moving to the United States. Many of these immigrants came from Ireland, Italy, England and other countries looking for a new place to call home. New York City was where many of these people ended up. Because of all the people, New York City was a busy, noisy place with many factories, stores and crowded streets.

Close your eyes and imagine yourself standing on a street in New York City at this time. You hear people walking and talking and horses trotting down the dirt roads. You smell freshly baked bread being sold on a corner; a whistle blows as work starts in a nearby factory. Men wear vests and caps, women wear dresses.

As you walk down the street you hear a boy calling from the corner. He is shouting loudly. You turn and walk toward him. You see that he is a small boy, with old, grimy clothes and holes in his shoes. He's carrying a larger stack of newspapers and holding one high over his head.

"Read the headlines, Spanish-American War rages on!" The boy waves a paper at you. "Do you want to buy a paper?" he asks. You nod and give him a coin and he hands you a newspaper. You look at the newspaper, the top of it reads "Spanish-American War" in big bold letters. You read about a war with pictures of ships sailing across the ocean and soldiers marching.

The boy who sold you the newspaper was called a newsboy. In New York City there were many young boys who didn't have families; or often they had families, but were very poor and needed them to work. The newsboys woke up early in the morning and hurried to the printer where they bought newspapers. Then they would carry their papers through the city and do whatever they could to sell these newspapers to make a little extra money. It wasn't an easy life, but they did what they could to stay alive. Sometimes being a newsboy was dangerous as sometimes the boys fought over who could have the best corner in the city. The roads were also very dangerous with horses and carriages.

During the Spanish-American War it was easy for the newsboys to sell their papers, because everyone wanted to know what was going on during the war. There were many newspaper companies in the city, but the two largest ones were called The World, which owned by Joseph Pulitzer, and The Journal, which was owned by William Randolph Hearst. During the war Pulitzer and Hearst increased the cost of their newspapers, because everyone wanted the news so badly so they were fine paying more for them. Pulitzer and Hearst also competed for better journalists and cartoonists. Newspapers were very popular at the time because there was no other way to get the news like the TV or Internet today. Often the newspapers made up stories to get more people to buy them. This wasn't very honest and was called "Yellow Journalism."

When the Spanish-American War ended less people bought newspapers so it became very hard for the newsboys to sell them. No matter how hard they tried to sell their papers, everyone wasn't as interested as before. On top of this, the newspaper owners made the papers more expensive, so people weren't as willing to buy them.

The newsboys knew if they wanted to stay alive they would need to come up with a plan to change the newspaper companies' minds. But newspaper owners like Joseph Pulitzer and William Randolph Hearst were very powerful men with lots of money, so to go against them would take a lot of hard work and determination.

One popular newsboy was named Louis Ballett, but everyone called him Kid Blink, because he had a patch over one of his eyes. Kid Blink and other newsboys decided to band together and not sell newspapers. If enough newsboys joined them they thought Pulitzer and Hearst might change their minds. This is called a strike. Kid Blink and other newsboys told other boys about their plan and soon none of the boys in New York City were selling papers. This was hard for the boys because if they weren't making any money, they didn't have food to eat. But they were determined to make a difference.

During one day of the strike, all the boys gathered on Brooklyn Bridge. There were so many newsboys that even the traffic had to stop! People all over New York City saw what the newsboys were doing and wanted to help them. They decided they wouldn't buy newspapers from Pulitzer and Hearst either. Pulitzer and Hearst tried to hire older men to sell their papers but no one would help, because they believed in the newsboys cause. Kid Blink and his friends kept giving speeches. In one speech Kid Blink said: “"Friens and feller workers. This is a time which tries de hearts of men. Dis is de time when we'se got to stick together like glue.... We know wot we wants and we'll git it even if we is blind."

After many days the newspaper companies were losing so much money they had no choice but to change what they were doing. They decided that instead of making the boys buy all of the papers, at the end of the day they would buy back what they hadn't sold. Finally the strike was over and the newsboys could go back to selling papers. Everyone was amazed that a group of small boys could change the minds of such powerful men such as Pulitzer and Hearst. Because of what these boys did many other workers striked. Sometimes it is necessary to strike if people need better places to work or deserve better pay. It's one way to keep a balance between workers and company owners. The Newsboys Strike of 1899 became an important part of workers rights history.

Like the newsboys, it's important to learn how to work when you are still small. You may not be working on the streets like they did, but you can help around your house and in the yard, pick up your toys, do the dishes, or do other helpful chores. Also, when you aren't treated with respect like the newsboys you can stand up for yourselves. Everyone deserves respect and to be treated well, no matter their size. Be sure to speak up and stand up for what is right even when it takes courage and is hard to do.

Stars

A History

Imagine you are standing in a wide open field. In the field you see a gigantic white rocket reaching far up into the sky. As you walk up to the rocket, the door opens and you climb inside and find a seat and buckle up. Next you hear the countdown: 5, 4, 3, 2, 1. Suddenly the rocket rumbles as it lifts of the ground and shoots through the sky, past the clouds, and up, up, up into space. When you look out the window you see the round blue ball of earth far below.

The rocket is going faster and faster. You zoom past the moon as the rocket picks up speed. Soon the other planets of our solar system pass you by. You look back and notice the earth has grown smaller and smaller until it has disappeared from view. Then suddenly you are traveling at the speed of light, and before long you have left the solar system and are deep into outer space. All is black. You travel further and further until suddenly you look out your window and see a beautiful cloud of dust and gas all swirling together. You have arrived at the place where stars are born. It is called a stellar nursery, which means a star birthing place.

Stars are sort of like people in that they are born, and they grow until they are bigger, and then eventually get old and die. But unlike people stars live for millions or even trillions of years. Our own sun is a star, it's just a lot closer than the stars we see twinkling in the sky at night that appear so small.

For millions of years clouds of dust and gas in space swirl around each other in what is called a nebula. Over time these clouds slowly group together into clumps that eventually become baby stars — or protostars. Some stars grow bigger and bigger until they become as large as our own sun. And often they have their very own planets, just like our sun has its own planets. These stars become very hot and bright, which is why when you look up at the sky at night you can see them even though they are sooo far away. To travel to many of these stars would take thousands of years.

The reason we know a lot about how stars are born is because of a space telescope. A space telescope is a telescope that is launched into space and can see better because it is above the earth. The Herschel Space Observatory was built by the European Space Agency and watched where stars were born for 4 years. Because of the hard work of the engineers and astronomers working on this space telescope, we know a lot more about the life of stars.

After changing from clouds of gas and dust many of these baby stars eventually become "main sequence" stars, then sub-giant stars and then red giant stars. Many of these very large stars are thousands of times bigger than our own sun. And our own sun is very, very big.

After millions of years even stars grow old and die. Eventually they begin to collapse in on themselves and then suddenly explode in what is called a supernova. During a supernova they shoot gas and dust for millions of miles around them. Supernovas happen in the universe all the time but often it's hard for us to see them happening because there are so many stars and they are so far away. The people who study stars are called astronomers. Most astronomers thought the only way to see supernovae would be to use a large telescope run by many astronomers.

In Australia lived an amateur astronomer named Robert Evans. Robert had a normal job during the day, but at night his favorite thing to do was to go on his back porch and use his little telescope to watch the stars. Robert was interested in supernovas, when stars explode, but decided he didn't need all of the big telescopes to see them. So he started watching for supernovas on his own. For many nights Robert didn't see anything. But he kept watching and kept waiting, until he saw his first supernova. He was so excited. Over the years Robert has seen 42 supernovae! Which is an amazing achievement. Because Robert is very patient and very diligent he has been able to see when these gigantic stars explode all the way across the galaxy.

When we look out in the night sky we see many stars, but they are very far away. After the sun, the closest star is called Alpha Centauri. Alpha Centauri is 25 trillion miles away! This gives you a little bit of an idea of how large our galaxy is.

Stars like our sun are very important because they are like huge factories which give off energy and heat. They send this energy in the form of waves that travel all the way across space to Earth. There are many reasons our sun is important. First off, without it would always be night. If it was always night, it would be very hard to see! Also, trees would never grow, because trees need the sun's energy to grow. Without trees and other plants we wouldn't have oxygen to breath and animals wouldn't have food. And without animals and plants we wouldn't be able to eat either. We would all be in very big trouble! Also, the earth would become very very cold and everything would freeze. Even on hot days, we should be very grateful we have a sun that keeps planet Earth running smoothly.

Next time when you go outside and feel the warm sun on your skin, think about how the sun rays travelled 100 million miles to to make you warm. That's pretty amazing that an object sooo far away can make its way all the way to you and keep you warm and keep us all alive.

When we learn about how stars and our own sun it makes us grateful for nature and the world around us. And when we understand how important they are it reminds us to respect and take care of what we have. Take some time to think of the ways you can better take care of the Earth, whether it means picking up trash outside or not wasting water or planting flowers or a tree. There are many things around us in nature that we can be curious about and appreciate if we just take the time to notice them.

George Lucas

The Making of Star Wars

A long time ago, in a galaxy far far away... Well, not really that long ago, and on our same planet, actually, a boy named George Lucas was born in California. George was like many other boys in his day. He liked comic books and rock music and TV shows which were a very new thing in his time. His favorite TV shows were adventure stories with daring heroes who did extraordinary things. These heroes had names such as Buck Rogers and Flash Gordon.

In order to buy his favorite things, George did chores around the house to earn a weekly allowance. One of his chores was mowing the lawn. The only problem was the family lawn mower was old, so it could be a very difficult chore. But George had the idea to save up his weekly money and buy a new lawnmower, so the job would be easier! This is called an investment, saving money toward something that will help you later.

In high school George loved cars. When he was 16 his dad bought him a car, but made sure it was a slow car, because he knew George liked to drive too fast. But George wouldn't let that stop him from driving fast. He hung around car mechanics and garages and learned how to tinker with car engines, until he figured out how to make his little car drive faster.

One of George's favorite things to do was to drive around town in his car with his friends. He also liked to race other boys in his car. He enjoyed this so much that someday he wanted to be a race car driver. But one day when George was driving home he was driving very fast and very dangerous. Suddenly his car flipped over and rolled three times. George's seat belt broke and he was thrown out of the car, just before his car smashed into a tree. An ambulance rushed George to the hospital. He was so hurt they didn't know if he would survive. But miraculously he lived and after a couple months in the hospital, George got better. George decided being a race car driver wasn't the best idea, so began looking for a new passion.

At school George started doing photography, which means taking pictures. He also decided to take classes to learn about filmmaking. A filmmaker is someone who makes movies. George made short movies and people really liked them. He had an eye for making movies look good and coming up with interesting ideas. His first big movie was about teenagers racing cars. It was called American Graffiti and to George's surprise it won many awards and made him a lot of money.

With all of the money from this movie he started to work on his next movie. He remembered all of the TV shows he loved growing up about adventures and space, and thought it would be fun to make a movie like that. His friends told him he should do a more serious movie, but with all of the sad things going on in the world like the Vietnam War, George wanted to do a more positive and fun movie.

So George started to think up names of his heroes and the places they lived. He imagined distant planets and adventures for his heroes. He dreamed up space battles where ships flew through space and shot lasers at each other. He invented strange aliens and other creatures and made notes about their names and personalities. He would call his movie The Star Wars.

After George wrote down all of the ideas, he needed to find a movie company who would pay for the movie. Many of the big companies thought it wasn't a good idea. They thought The Star Wars was silly and no one would watch it. But George kept trying until he found a movie company called 20th Century Fox that liked his idea and would give him the money to make The Star Wars.

Next George Lucas and his friends went to work improving his story. It took them many months of trying new characters and stories. Sometimes George got very bored with the work. Many times he had to go to different friends or his helpful wife to get new ideas. After a lot of work and patience he finally had a finished story for Star Wars. It would be about a young farm boy named Luke Skywalker who would meet an old Jedi named Obi Wan Kenobi. Together they would find a smuggler named Han Solo, who would help them return the missing droid R2D2 to its owner Princess Leia and rescue her from the evil Darth Vader.

Once the story was approved, George and his team found people to play the parts of their main characters, called actors. He also had a team of artists to turn his ideas into drawings so they could begin to make real costumes and ships and other props for the movie. When filming the spaceships nothing had been done like this before, so they had to be very creative and invent new ways to film the space battles to make them look real.

George and his crew had to travel to deserts and other places across the world to film all of the places for their movie. Unexpected challenges with filming, with the crew and with 20th Century Fox didn't leave George enough to make the movie, so he had to be creative and find ways to do things for less. By the time the movie was done, George wasn't sure if anyone would like it.

Finally, Star Wars was in theaters and audiences got to watch it for the first time. At the beginning when the music and the first space ship appeared on the screen everyone cheered. At the end of the movie the audience clapped and cheered and didn't stop. They loved it! They were so amazed at what they saw. Nothing like Star Wars had ever been done before! People went back and saw it over and over. Many stood in line for hours just to see it again. George knew he had made a great movie, but had no idea how much people would love it. It became a box office hit, broke many records, and was the most popular movie for many years all over the world.

All of George and his team's hard work and creativity finally paid off. They went on to make two more Star Wars movies, The Empire Strikes Back and Return of the Jedi. Both movies were also very popular.

A few years later George dreamed up a new hero, an archeologist who went on adventures. He named after his own dog, Indiana, and Indiana Jones was born. George made this movie with his friend Steven Spielberg and it was also a huge success.

More recently, Disney bought the rights to Star Wars from George Lucas for four billion dollars. George said he would give half of the money to people in need. Much of it will go to helping schools.

George Lucas wasn't afraid to try new things and use his imagination and creativity to come up with new ideas. Often our creative ideas can lead to new and exciting things. If you ever have an idea be sure to write it down, make your own story, or draw a picture of it. George's ideas sparked the imagination of millions, and got many young people interested in space and making their own movies.

Watching movies is a helpful way to relax our brains and open them up to new ideas. Spend some time thinking about what you might do to be creative, because you never know what your own ideas will lead to!

Nancy Wake

World War Commando

Close your eyes and imagine you are a soldier flying in a plane high above the ocean. Outside you hear the plane's propellers turning and strong winds rushing past the windows. It is the middle of the night and down below the ocean is dark and cold. Sitting around you are other soldiers, men and women with dark clothes and large backpacks. They look nervous and you feel nervous too. You check your gun and tighten a parachute which is also on your back.

The year is 1944 and you are in the middle of World War 2. Nazi Germany has invaded France. France's allies England and the United States and other countries are working to help France and many other countries be free again. If the battle can be won in France there might be a chance to beat the Nazis and make the world a safe place again. You look around at the other soldiers, but remember you and the others here are no ordinary soldiers. You are part of England's Special Operations Executive, commandos which are a combination of a soldier and a spy. You have trained many months to be a commando and it's finally your chance to help the people of France.

"Everyone ready?" a voice calls from the back of the plane. You look out the window and see that you are above land now. This is France. You and the other soldiers stand up and walk toward the back of the plane. In the front you see one of the most famous commandos -- a woman named Nancy Wake. The back doors to the plane open.

You watch as Nancy walks to the back of the plane and jumps out into the cold night. Soon you jump out, too, and are are falling down, down toward the ground. At the right moment you pull your parachute and are yanked up into the sky. You look across the French countryside and float downward until your boots hit the ground and you roll, then hurriedly wrap up your parachute.

Nancy Wake and the other commandos are running low across a grassy field to the cover of trees. Someone whispers that a German patrol is nearby. You quietly hurry on until you are hidden deep in the woods. Everyone huddles together and pulls out their backpacks. You see that Nancy is safe and are glad to have such a brave woman leading your team. You know with her help you can accomplish your dangerous and very important mission.

Nancy Wake was born in Wellington, New Zealand. A couple years later her family moved to Australia. There she went to school until the age of 16 when she left home and found a job as a nurse. Working as a nurse, she was able to save some money and with the help of an aunt, was bought a plane ticket to New York City. There she learned how to become a journalist. A journalist is someone who writes stories for the newspaper. To Nancy being a journalist was an adventure. She loved to travel and learn about new people and places. One of the places she visited was Austria. While she was in Austria a powerful leader named Adolf Hitler had become very powerful. Hitler's country of Germany was nearby Austria. In Austria

Hitler's followers, the Nazis, were hurting people they did not like, such as the Jews. When Nancy saw how horribly the Nazis treated these people, she realized Hitler was very dangerous.

Nancy moved to Paris, France one of her favorite places in the world. She loved the city and the people and eventually married a Frenchman named Henri Edmond Fiocca. While Nancy was living in France, Hitler's army invaded the country. Hitler wanted to control France, but Nancy did everything to try and stop him. She joined a group called The Resistance. She helped soldiers escape France and sent secret messages to help The Resistance. Nancy was very careful, so for a long time the Nazis didn't know she was a spy. She was very sneaky and for this reason the Nazis called her "The White Mouse." Her job was very dangerous, but Nancy knew that fighting against the invaders was the right thing to do, so she did it anyway. The Nazis wanted to catch Nancy so badly that they offered 5 million French dollars to anyone who would turn her in.

Soon it was too dangerous for Nancy to stay in France, so she snuck out of the country, hiding in the back of a coal truck, just before the Nazis caught her. From France she went to Spain and then to England, which was a country safe from the Nazis. Nancy could have lived a safe life in England far from her enemies, but she knew she needed to keep fighting to keep the world free. In England Nancy joined England's spy group called the Special

Operations Executive. There Nancy trained to be a soldier and a spy, also known as a commando. She learned to shoot a gun, use a radio, and be sneaky, which she was already pretty good at. But Nancy worked very hard and tried to be very cheerful. When other soldiers were sad she made funny jokes and cheered them up. The other soldiers like to be around Nancy.

Once Nancy and the other soldiers were trained, a plane flew them across the ocean to France where they jumped out and parachuted down to the ground. Many Nazis were in France so they were careful and spent much of the time in hiding. There Nancy and the other soldiers helped The Resistance. They gave them guns and other supplies, blew up bridges, recruited more people to the Resistance. Once they even attacked a Nazi base. Nancy and the other commandos weren't afraid to complete dangerous missions to help free the people of France.

To keep in touch with England the commandos used radio and special codes. One night the codes were destroyed by the enemy and the next closest radio station was very far away. Many would have given up, but Nancy decided she could ride a bike to the other radio. So she jumped on her bike and rode almost 200 miles. She had to pass many Nazis along the way, so it was a very dangerous journey, but Nancy was brave and believed in her cause. After delivering the message to be sent, Nancy got back on her bike and rode all the way back to her team.

While Nancy and the other commandos were helping The Resistance, the Allied Armies fought Hitler's army on the battlefield until chasing them out of France. Nancy was excited to see France free again and proud to have been one of many to make it happen.

After the war Nancy received many medals for her bravery. Later she wrote a book about her life and adventures during the war and called it "The White Mouse." Nancy moved into a hotel in France where the owners and others helped take care of her, because of all she had done to help their country. Nancy Wake's bravery inspired many women and men for years to come.

Like Nancy, you can do things even when you're not sure how they'll turn out. Sometimes we only want to do the things we know about -- this is called staying inside our comfort zone. But it's also good for us to get outside of our comfort zone and try new things like Nancy did. We can stand up for what we believe even when it might be scary. If you see someone picking on someone else, you can tell them this is wrong and stand up for them. You might wonder if you can be as brave as Nancy, but remember she was once a child just like you.

Nellie Blye

Around the World in 72 Days

Close your eyes and imagine leaving your home and traveling all the way around the world. You would cross oceans, meet new people, try new foods, and see new places. It would be an exciting journey, even dangerous at times, but it would change the way you see everything. Nellie Blye is a woman who did just that -- and finished the journey faster than anyone else in the world.

Nellie Blye was born in 1864 and lived in a time when kids didn't go to school most of the day. Instead they worked long days. Nellie had a big family with *fifteen* brothers and sisters who all worked in their father's mill. A mill is a place where wheat is ground into flour to make bread. Here she learned to work hard and have determination. Determination is trying your best and not giving up until you finish something.

Nellie loved to wear the color pink. One day her friend said, "You wear pink so much, we're going to call you 'pinky'!" From then on she had the nickname "pinky."

Nellie also loved to write. She practiced writing and as a result became very good at it. When she got a little older, she became a journalist. A journalist is someone who writes for the newspaper. Nellie was also very curious and loved learning about new things. She wrote about the new things she learned in the newspaper. Her stories soon made her very famous.

One day Nellie was reading a book called “Around the World in 80 Days” by Jules Verne about a man who travelled around the world. Even though the book wasn’t a true story, Nellie wanted to do it herself -- and she believed she could. Other people told her it would be too dangerous, or that because she was a girl she couldn’t do it. They told her she needed someone strong to protect her. But Nellie was independent and brave and believed she could do it on her own.

So Nellie packed her clothes and other things into a bag and went to the dock where the ship was waiting. Everyone cheered and waved “good-bye” as the ship set sail. At sea Nellie became very sea sick. Sea sick is when someone not used to the ocean gets very sick from the boat rocking in the water. But even though it was hard she was sick she kept going, she was determined to finish the journey.

Next, the ship landed in England, from here she went to France and finally to Asia. Sometimes she travelled by boat, someones by train. She tasted new foods, went alligator hunting, bought a monkey, and rode ponies across Hong Kong. Newspapers all over the world kept track of Nellie Blye. Everyone was watching to see how fast she finished her trip.

After returning to America, Nellie travelled across the country and people waved to her along the way, gave her flowers and fruit, and shook her hand. Girls and boys saw what Nellie was doing and realized they could do difficult things, too.

By the time she got home, she had travelled 25,000 miles in 72 days. It was a *very long* trip and she was tired and glad to be home. Because Nellie was brave and believed in herself, other women saw that they could do adventurous things too. She was an inspiration to all.

Like Nellie, you can learn to work and be determined -- to keep trying and trying and not give up even when something is difficult. You can also be curious. You can imagine new things and do them even when others doubt in you or no one else has done them before. It may take learning new things and lots of practice and courage, but you can do it if you keep trying.

Mahatma Ghandi

Faithful Leader of Peace

Have you heard ever heard of a country called India? India is between China and the Middle East and much of it is surrounded by the Indian Ocean. India is home to one of the world's oldest civilizations and for many years was one of the richest countries in the world. Over one billion people live in India. It has more people than any other country in the world, second only to China.

In the 1800s the British Empire ruled many countries of the world including America. During the American Revolution the Patriots fought off the British King and his soldiers and became their own free country. At the time of our story the British Empire was still in control of India. This is the story of how India came to be free and the man who helped make it happen.

In 1869 in the city of Porbander, India a boy named Mahandas Ghandi was born in a small home to a simple family. The Ghandis were good people. The father was a leader in the city and his mother was a very religious woman. She taught her children to pray and read scriptures such as the Bhagavad Gita, the Vegas, and some texts from the Bible and Quaran. The Ghandis were Hindu, so they didn't drinking wine or eat meat. Ghandi's mother also taught the family to fast -- which means going without food for a certain period of time. She believed it gave them strength and self control.

When Mahandas was little he was very playful and sometimes liked to cause trouble. Often he would chase down dogs and twist their ears. He also loved to listen to classic Indian stories, such as the stories of Shravan and Harischandra, which were epic tales about virtue and adventure. These stories taught good principles and helped Mahandas want to be a good person.

At age nine Mahandas started school and there learned math, history, language and geography. He was just an okay student and pretty shy and had trouble speaking. This made him very nervous when he had to speak in front of his class, but he did like books and learning.

At this time in India people got married very young. Mahandas was 13 when he married a girl named Kasturba. When Kasturba was 17 they had their first baby, but sadly she didn't live very long. This same year Mahandas also lost his father, so it was a very hard time for him. But later Mahandas and Kasturba had four more children, so it made them happy to be parents.

Next Ghandi decided to travel to London, the capital of the British Empire, to go to college to become a lawyer. A lawyer is someone who helps others work with thc law, the rules that keep a country in order. Ghandi's parents were worried while he was there he wouldn't live his religion, that he would eat meat and drink alcohol and do other things they didn't approve of. But when he left he promised them he would stay faithful no matter what. And Ghandi did live up to his word, he stayed strong in his Hindu religion while he was away from home. This is called commitment and dedication to something you believe in.

Ghandi learned a lot about the English people while he was in London. He had always been shy and at first school was difficult, but instead of giving up he joined a group that taught him how to speak louder and more clearly and with lots of practice he became a very good speaker.

After finishing college, Ghandi got a job working for a shipping company in South Africa. At this time the British Empire also ruled South Africa. In South Africa Ghandi was treated badly by the English because he was from India. Once when he was on a train they didn't let him sit with other people. They picked him up and threw him off the train. Ghandi was so upset by this he refused to leave the train station until they let him on the next train. This is called a protest. Finally, they let Ghandi back on the train. Many times Ghandi was treated badly because he was from India. He started to think England shouldn't be in control of India anymore.

When Ghandi moved back to India and he was determined to do everything he could to make India a free country. He began speaking and writing about what the India people needed to do to become free. But Ghandi was a peaceful person and didn't believe in hurting others to become free. Instead they would peacefully protest and use civil disobedience -- which means finding other ways to make your point other than violence.

One thing England did to control India was tax the things they bought, this meant charging extra for food and clothes and keeping the money. So instead of buying clothes and salt from England, Ghandi decided to make his own clothes and salt. He learned how to make his own clothes and started wearing them. Thousands of other India people started doing the same. This made the British upset, because they were losing money. To make his own salt, Ghandi began a journey to the ocean. He walked over 200 miles to make salt in the ocean. People all over India followed him and did the same. All across the world people saw what Ghandi and the India people were doing and sympathized with them. Ghandi was put in jail many times for his actions. He would go without eating until they would set him free. What Ghandi was doing was very difficult, but he was sacrificing his owns desires for the country and people he loved.

Sometimes the Indian people wanted to use guns and weapons to fight the British leaders, but Ghandi continually taught that this was the wrong way. He used scriptures of many different religions to show that peace was a better way. When his people did start to fight Ghandi would go without eating for many days until they stopped. The people often stopped because they loved Ghandi and didn't want him to be hungry.

Eventually, England let India become free. The amazing part of this story is that it came about without a big war and lots of people dying. This was truly a miracle and Ghandi showed the world that freedom can come about through peaceful ways. The Indian people and Ghandi celebrated. They were so happy to be in control of their own country. The time after this was very challenging as they figured out how to be on their own, but it gave them a chance to make their own choices and be a free people.

Not long after India became free Ghandi passed away, but his mission was complete and the Indian people and people all across the world will remember him as someone who loved his people and gave his life for them.

In life it's easy to focus on yourself and what makes you happy. Its natural for us to want to take care of ourselves, which is important to some degree. But giving of ourselves to help others is also very important. It's important to share and to think about what makes others happy. Spend some time thinking about what makes others happy and then do something about it. Next time you have a treat think about how happy it will make others to taste it, too. If you are playing with a toy, think about how your brother or sister or friend might enjoy playing with it.

Ghandi believed in being peaceful. Next time someone wants to fight with you or argue, think about a more peaceful way you can deal with the problem. You never know, in the end someone who you think is an enemy might become a friend.

Sacajawea

Noble Explorer

A long time ago, in the 1800s, the United States was still a young country. At this time much of the wilderness hadn't been explored by the new Americans yet. This land was inhabited by Indians and many animals and nature was still fresh and dangerous and wild. The new Americans were curious about this land and wanted to know what plants and animals were there. Most importantly they wanted to know how to best travel from the East Coast to the West Coast.

In 1803 President Thomas Jefferson bought this land from France in what was known as the Louisiana Purchase. Next, he asked one of his captains, Meriwether Lewis, to discover this new land and make a record of what was there. It would be a dangerous mission, but Lewis was brave and bold and loved discovering new places. Captain Lewis asked his friend Lieutenant William Clark to go with him. So they gathered their team and their supplies, climbed into a boat, and headed down the river to discover the uncharted American wilderness.

A few years before this a little Indian girl was born far across the country near the Rocky Mountains. Her parents named her Sacajawea. Her people were called the

Shoshone and they lived among the trees and wild animals, and learned how to live off the land and hunt like many other Indian families. Sacajawea felt safe in this place and loved her family.

When Sacajawea was 12 years old her tribe was attacked by another tribe. A frightening battle took place and afterward Sacajawea and many other girls were kidnapped by their enemies. As she was lifted onto their horse and carried away she didn't know if she'd ever see her family again. This was a very scary time for Sacajawea.

A few years later Sacajawea was sold to a trapper named Charbonneau and later became his wife. A trapper is someone who traps animals and lives off selling their fur and meat.

As Captain Lewis and Clark were exploring the wilderness they needed someone who was familiar with the land and the language, so when they met Charbonneau and Sacajawea they knew she would be a perfect fit.

Not long after they Sacajawea joined Lewis and Clark, she gave birth to a baby boy who she named him Jean Baptiste, but Lewis and Clark liked to call him "Little Pompy." For the rest of the journey she would travel with her baby boy tied to her back.

The journey down the river was often very dangerous. One day when they were riding through rough water, the boat suddenly collapsed and everyone and their things dropped into the water. After everyone swam to shore, Lewis realized their precious journals were missing.

These journals were very important because they were a record of everything they had seen and done. Knowing this, Sacajawea bravely dove into the water and swam deep down until she found the journal on the bottom of the river. Lewis was so relieved when Sacajawea swam back to the shore with his journals.

Sacajawea was helpful because she knew the plants and animals of this wild land. She would cook up roots for them to eat and show them the way when they were lost. She was also a peaceful ambassador to the other Indians. An ambassador is someone who tries to help two different groups of people talk to each other and make peace. Sacajawea knew the Indian languages and kept Lewis and Clark and their crew safe.

Far along in their journey, they met some Indians and asked them if they could trade horses. At first the Indians would not trade. Suddenly Sacajawea recognized them, they were Shoshones, the tribe she had been kidnapped from so long ago! And to her surprise the chief was her brother. She was so happy to see her friends and family again. After celebrating with her tribe, she helped Lewis and Clark trade some of their things for horses, and although she was sad to leave her family, they were on their way again. She had a new family and a new mission to complete.

Finally, after many days crossing rivers and forests and mountains the team reached the Pacific Ocean, the end of their journey. With the help of Sacajawea, Lewis and

Clark had traveled over 3700 miles! Along the way they had learned new things about the land and plants and animals and made maps that would help pioneers and other Americans journey across the country.

Like Sacajawea, you can be helpful to others and be brave even when you're not sure about how your journey will go. Also, you can be strong even when sad or difficult things happen to you. It's okay to feel sad, but always remember that after you've let all your feelings out, you can stand back up, continue on, and learn something new. No matter what happens there is always hope and good things will come when you keep moving forward!

Abraham Lincoln

From a Log Cabin to Defender of the Union

Abraham Lincoln was born in 1809 in Kentucky to parents who were very poor at the time. They lived in the middle of the woods in a very small log cabin his father built. The woods were full of wild animals and no one else lived nearby. Every night Abe and his family slept on a hard dirt floor.

When Abe was old enough to work, everyday he and his father, Thomas, ate a small breakfast, picked up their axes, and ventured off into the thick woods to chop down trees to make the land flat for farming. It was very hard work and they worked all day long. Abe became very strong chopping wood. He also began to grow very tall for his age. He grew so much that his pants became too small and because his parents were poor they couldn't afford to buy him new ones. Some people thought he looked funny because he was so tall and skinny, but they liked Abe because he was kind and funny.

In Abe's town there wasn't a school, so most days he just worked. For a short time a teacher lived a few miles away so Abraham did learn a little, but just enough to read and write. Once Abe learned to read it became his favorite thing to do. He only had a couple books, but he spent any free time he had reading. When he learned something new he repeated the words over and over until he knew them by memory. He also wrote new words down. This helped him remember the words so he could use them later.

After Abe and his father cleared the land of trees, they began farming. Most days he'd take a book out to the field and read in between planting. His mother, Nancy, read to him and his sister. She knew learning was very important and taught Abe this from a young age. Abe loved his mother very much.

When Abe was only nine his mother became sick and died. He and his family were very sad. Not long after this, his father left him and his sister for *nine months* while he went to find a new wife. Can you imagine being left alone for that long? Somehow Abraham survived, finding help from caring neighbors. Eventually, his father returned with their new mother. When Abe saw on the road he ran and hugged her, even though he didn't know her. He was just happy to have a mother again.

Sarah turned out to be a very good mother to Abe. She found him new books and was kind to him. Abe's father Thomas was hard on him. He was also known to be a very good storyteller. This was a talent Abe picked up and was known for later in his life.

Once Abraham was old enough to be on his own, he left home and started working for himself. He knew that by working hard, he could improve his life. He had a job moving goods down the river, then later worked in a store. Once while working in the store, someone paid the wrong amount of money. That night Abe walked very far to return the money. This is where he got his nickname "Honest Abe." Honesty means telling the truth.

One day in town Abe went to the courthouse and saw a lawyer arguing a case. A lawyer is someone who understands the law and often helps defends others when they need something. When Abe heard the lawyer speaking, he decided being a lawyer was what he wanted to do. Without going to a big school, Abraham read and studied and repeated words on his own until he knew everything he needed to to become a lawyer. This took lots of time and practice but soon he became very smart and understood the law. He passed all the tests he needed and before long became a lawyer. He traveled from town to town on his horse helping others.

While working as a lawyer, Abe became interested in politics. Politics involves law and government and voting in new leaders. Abe wanted to become a leader so he could shape and change the country for the better. His first job in the state government was the House of Representatives. Later, he was part of the U.S. House of Representatives. There he helped pass laws to build railroads and support banks so the state could grow and improve.

At the same time slavery was a tragic problem in United States. Slavery is when someone is forced to work without any pay. Many Americans had slaves that they treated very poorly and made them work very hard. Abe knew slavery was horrible and was against slavery it spreading to the new states in America. He argued this against another leader named Stephen A. Douglas. These arguments became very intense at times, because Americans were very upset about slavery, either being for it or against it.

At this time Abe ran for President of the United States. Many Americans in the South were against Abe being president, because they wanted to keep slavery. Also, many Americans thought Abe could never win because he was just a farm boy from the woods who didn't have very much money or schooling. But Abe cared about helping the country and to everyone's surprise he won and became the President of the United States! The people who loved Abe were very excited that such a caring man had become their new president.

But Southerners who wanted to keep slavery were angry and wanted to break off from America. They said they would form a new country where they could keep their slaves. This was called The Civil War, because it was a war between two parts of our country, the North and the South. Soon very dangerous fighting began and many soldiers on both sides died. It was a very sad time for the United States.

Abraham Lincoln wanted more than anything to keep the country together. He believed America was stronger and better as one country. But he was also very sad to see soldiers dying on both sides. Some wanted to quit the fight, but Abe was determined to not give up. He gave the Gettysburg Address and his bold words inspired Americans to follow him. He also worked to create new laws to stop slavery even when it was unpopular to do so.

Finally, the war came to an end when General Robert E. Lee surrendered to the North. It was a time of much celebration for the North. Many lives had been lost, but in the end the country stayed together and the slaves became free. Some leaders may have been harsh to the losing side of the war, but Abraham Lincoln was determined to show kindness and mercy to the South and do all he could to rebuild the broken country.

Not long after the war ended, while Abe was watching a play at Ford's Theater, he was shot by the assassin John Wilkes Booth. The Americans who loved Abe were very sad at this news. They had lost the president who cared for them and saved the country. But having done all he could, Abraham Lincoln has gone down in history as one of the greatest presidents of all time.

Like Abe, no matter where you were born or to whom, you can decide to improve yourself and be a good person. Abe had very little, but he read everything he could and studied and worked until he could make a living for himself. He also decided to help his country by running for different offices in the government. These aren't easy jobs, but when good people lead they can make a great difference. Like Abe, you can be aware of what is going on in your own communities and in your country. And when you're old enough you can vote for good leaders and even become one yourself. Just remember, no matter your circumstances, if you make the decision to improve yourself and do good things, you can do it!

The Navy SEALs

America's Elite Fighting Force

In the 1960s, during the Vietnam War, the United States military began to train special soldiers who could move about secretly in small teams and complete special missions. This was the beginning of the Navy SEALs.

Any man or woman who wants to become a Navy must first join the Navy. Then they must pass tests to be sure they are ready for BUD/S training. BUD/S Training is a very difficult camp where leaders decide who is ready to be a Navy SEAL. There they run through wet sand with all their clothes on, crawl through deep mud, and carry heavy rubber boats. They do lots of situps and pushups and plenty of running. Most days they get very little sleep and have to swim far out in the ocean, and hold their breath underwater for a very long time. Not only do their bodies have to be strong, but their minds as well. They have to be able to keep going and going even when their body and mind want to give up.

People who want to become Navy SEALs spend many years training before they even go to BUD/S Training. Because it is so hard many aren't able to finish. This doesn't mean they are weak, it is just a very great challenge to become a Navy SEAL.

At the end of boot camp, SEALs start other training, such as learning how to scuba dive under the water and how to parachute out of very high airplanes. They also learn how to shoot guns and set off bombs. The word SEAL is the words "sea", "air", and "land" all together. This means a SEAL needs to be able to move across sea, air and land to accomplish their special missions.

SEAL training can last up to a year, but even when they are done they keep practicing and practicing. A Navy SEAL is never fully done learning and improving.

At the end of their first training, the trainees are given a gold badge that has an eagle on it, which they can pin to their Navy uniform. It is a very exciting day, because they have worked so hard and so long to reach their goal.

Once a Navy SEAL completes their training they are assigned to a team. That team may live anywhere in the world, because their mission may take place anywhere in the world; and they need to be close and ready when they are needed.

When a mission takes place the Navy SEALs may arrive there by airplane, where they parachute down, or it might be by boat or helicopter or even by submarine if they are scuba swimming to their mission. They wear camouflage clothes depending on where the missions is, since it may be in the desert or the jungle or in a city.

The Navy SEALs have assisted in many wars in the past and are active today in places like the Middle East. Their mission might be to capture an enemy or to rescue someone who has been kidnapped. SEALs are very fast and skilled at what they do and can get in and out of places very fast. During one mission their job was to stop modern day pirates who had captured a big ship and its crew. For another mission they rescued soldiers who had been captured by the enemy.

Often Navy SEALs have to sacrifice their own lives when they go on these dangerous missions. In 2005 during the Afghanistan War, a 4-man team of SEALs landed by helicopter in an enemy area. Their job was to capture a dangerous Taliban leader. The members of this team were Lieutenant Michael Murphy and Petty Officers Marcus Luttrell, Danny Dietz and Matt Axelson.

While sneaking through enemy territory, the team ran into a boy and his father herding goats. The team decided to let them live and after they let them go, the father alerted the enemy and soon the team was being attacked Marcus from all sides. The SEALs fought for a very long time and tried to survive, but soon only Marcus Luttrell was left alive.

Marcus was strong and kept fighting and running until he was taken in by a friendly villager who lived nearby.

Sometimes it's not easy to know who is a friend or enemy in war, but this family took care of Marcus until a Navy helicopter came and took him away. After arriving home, Marcus wrote a book about the battle of him and his team and called it "Lone Survivor."

Navy SEALs are in many ways ordinary people who want to make a change in the world and serve their country. Their job is never easy, but they practice long and hard to be very good at what they do.

Spend some time thinking about what you can do to improve yourself like a Navy SEAL. You don't have to become a Navy SEAL to make yourself strong or become better at something. It might just be playing outside instead of watching TV, or riding your bike, or swimming, or doing something kind for someone else. You can have the spirit of a Navy SEAL, which is to accomplish great things even when they take time, hard work and practice.

Sylvester Stallone

The Rocky Story

On July 6, 1946 a boy named Sylvester was born. When it was time for his mother to give birth Sylvester's body was not coming out easily. In order for him to survive they used special tools, which although they saved his life, caused part of his lip and face not to work right. Because of this he always had a funny smile and even talked funny.

Sylvester grew up in the big city of New York. Growing up wasn't easy there. His parents didn't get along and they had to move many times. At one point he had to live with different families until he was able to move back with his father. With all of this going on in his life, Sylvester had a tough time in school and didn't always do very well.

But Sylvester loved going to the movies. He in the theater and stared up at the gigantic screen as larger than life heroes did amazing things. He saw how strong and fast and courageous they were and wanted to be just like them. The problem was Sylvester realized he didn't look like those heroes. He was short and small and got teased for his smile. But this didn't stop Sylvester. He began to exercise and do pushups and run, and do anything to shape himself into the heroes he saw in the movies.

As Sylvester got older his love of movies made him want to become an actor, so he went to a school for actors. He tried his very best there until it was time to be done and look for a job. But finding an acting job isn't easy. Sylvester did all kinds of odd jobs on the side. He even cleaned lion cages at the zoo! But most of the time he didn't have any money and it was very hard to get by. So he could pay for food, Sylvester had to sell his favorite dog. He was very sad about this. But Sylvester was determined to become an actor so he sacrificed things for it.

One day Sylvester saw a boxing match on TV. The boxers were Muhammed Ali and Chuck Wepner. Even though Chuck was getting beat up pretty badly, he kept standing up and fighting back. Sylvester had an idea, so he rushed home and started writing. He wrote all night and all day until the story was done. Next, he took his story to the movie companies and they *loved* the boxer story. They said they would pay him $125,000 for the story. Sylvester said he would sell it, but on one condition -- that he would also be the star in the movie. The directors laughed at this. They thought Sylvester looked a little funny and talked funny. They kept offering Sylvester more money for the story, but he demanded that he be the star. He was persistent and believed in himself.

Finally, the movie directors said he could be the star, but they didn't pay him as much for the story. But Sylvester didn't care because he believed he could be the star. And one of the first things he did with the money was bought his old dog back!

When the movie was finished it was about a small boxer named Rocky who nobody knew. But the boxer exercised and practiced and worked very hard until in a big boxing match he beat one of the best boxers in the world! People loved the movie named Rocky! It even won many awards and became one of the most popular movies of all time. Sylvester went from being an unknown actor to starring in many big movies. He always worked hard playing his parts, and exercised and stayed strong and fast. Most of the time he wanted to do his own stunts, even though it was dangerous. Today Sylvester Stallone is known as one of the greatest action movie stars of all time.

Later in his life Sylvester tried to do good things with the money he earned from his movies. They held an auction to sell the boxing gloves and other items from his Rocky movie and made $3 million dollars which they gave to those in need.

Remember that becoming good at something requires a lot of practice and persistence. Persistence is when you keep trying and trying even when things aren't working out. Sylvester had a dream and stuck with it even when it wasn't working out. Sometimes dreams take time and courage and patience. Like the boxer Rocky we can keep getting back up and trying even when difficult things in life knock us down.

Kerri Strugg

Olympic Gymnast

Have you ever heard of the Olympic Games? The Olympics is a huge sporting event that happens once every two years, where countries from all over the world come together in one place to compete. It starts off with a big parade and is an exciting time for everyone in the world. A young girl named Kerri Strugg was an Olympian who competed in the games.

Kerri was born in Tucson, Arizona and started taking gymnastic classes when she was only 3 years old. She went to gymnastic practice very often and worked very hard at improving her skills. It wasn't always easy, but she loved gymnastics and wanted to be very good at it. She loved swinging on the bars and doing cartwheels and flips on the mats. And by the time she was 8, Kerri was competing against other gymnasts. Soon after this she started practicing very seriously with a special coach so she could go on to the great Olympics games. Her family even decided to move so she could practice with the best coach.

It probably wasn't easy moving schools, having to make new friends, but she was determined to reach her goal.

When Kerri was only 14 she went to her first Olympics in Barcelona Spain. She was the youngest girl on the team and got to fly far across the ocean with the rest of her team. At the Olympics they worked very hard and did their best and ended up winning a Bronze Medal -- which is a very great award, but it is 3rd place. More than anything she wanted to win a Gold Medal. But for many years the Gold Medal in gymnastics was won by the Russian and Romanian teams, who were very good.

In between Olympics, Kerri continued to practice every day. She continued to learn more and build stronger muscles and improve until she could be the best gymnast she could be. There were times she fell and got hurt and it was hard to get back up, but she had a goal in mind and kept going. One time she was swinging around a bar and hit another bar and it hurt her so badly she had to go to the hospital. It took a long time for her to train her body so she could compete again, but nothing stopped Kerri.

Around this time her coach from the first Olympics, Bela Karolyi, started to work with her again. She continued to do well in other competitions, preparing for the Olympics. But finally the Summer Olympic Games came again. This time it was in Atlanta Georgia, and Kerri joined her team of other gymnasts who became known as the Magnificent Seven. When Kerri got to the Olympics, she saw the Russian gymnasts and remembered how good they were.

They always seemed to win and Kerri and her friends wanted the Gold Medal so badly.

When the games began, the Russian gymnasts were doing very well. They had also trained very hard and also wanted the Gold Medal. For many days the Russians were receiving higher scores and Kerri and her team wondered if they could win. On the last day it was Kerri's turn and she ran as fast as she could across the mat, did a cartwheel, then a back-handspring and flipped several times and landed on the mat, but her feet didn't land right and she heard a "snap!" Then she fell and her ankle hurt very badly. She wanted to cry, but held it in and limped off the mat.

By this time the score was very close and she would have to do a flip one more time if she wanted her team to win the Gold Medal. But her foot hurt and she didn't know if she could do it.

"You can do it!" her coach, Bela said to her. "You can do it." Everyone was cheering her on. They believed she could do it again, even though she was in so much pain.

When it was her turn, Kerri took a deep breath, tried to forget the pain in her foot, and started at the beginning of the mat. She wanted to win so much. She knew she could do it. She heard the crowds cheering. She started running even though her foot hurt. She did another cartwheel and back hand spring and many flips. When she came down on the mat she landed with both feet! It was amazing! The crowd cheered wildly! She had done it! With her hurt ankle she had done the flip and landed on both feet! The judges gave her a very good score.

But this was all she could give and after raising her arms to the crowd and the judges, she fell down. Her coaches ran to her side, because they could see she was hurt. She was taken to the hospital so they could bandage her leg.

On the final day of the Olympics Kerri was carried out to the crowd by her coach, Bela, with her bandaged leg, and there she and her team listened to the Star Spangled Banner, America's song as they received Gold Medals. After all of their practice and hard work their dreams had come true!

This was Kerri's last Olympic Games, but as she got older she went on to do other good things that weren't in the news, but still important. She became an ice skater and also finished college. Kerri then went on to teach elementary school in California and later got married and became a mom to two kids.

Like Kerri, when we have goals we can work toward them. Every day we may need to do something to make them happen. We can dream and dream, but in order for those dreams to become true we have to do something about them, even if they are small. What you do doesn't always have to be in the news or make you famous, but if it's improving yourself or helping others around you, that is what is most important.

Benjamin Franklin

The First American

Have you heard of a Founding Father before? A Founding Father is someone who helped start the United States of America. Benjamin Franklin was a Founding Father. Some have also called him the First American, because he had so many of the traits that would become known as American, such as hard work and independence. Independence is when you do something for yourself.

Benjamin Franklin was born in Boston Massachusetts to a very large family. He had 17 brothers and sisters! His family didn't have very much money so he only went to school for 2 years. But he did spend a lot of time reading on his own. He also learned to write and enjoyed doing it.

When he was young he worked for his older brother who was a printer. A printer would print newspapers and books for other people. Printing was important, because it was the best way to share an idea at that time. Printers would use little metal letters and build entire pages of words and sentences, then use black ink to make copies of the metal letters. Because Ben was working for his older brother he was called an “apprentice.” An apprentice is someone who is learning to become a master at a certain skill like printing.

While Ben was working as a printer he also liked to write for the newspaper. He would use a fake name Silence Dogood to write in the newspaper. He pretended to be an old lady and wrote funny jokes. Many people in the town thought this was very funny and didn’t know it was Ben writing the jokes.

After a few years Ben left his brother’s shop and started working for a new printer. His job was to set the metal letters in the big printing machine. He was also a clerk, a shopkeeper and a bookkeeper. He liked to stay busy and to learn all he could while he was working.

Around this time, when he was 20 years old, Ben formed a group including other Americans who also liked to read. Books cost a lot of money to buy, and there were no libraries, so Ben and his friends started their own library. They shared the books they read and met together to talk about what they read. Later in his life Ben would help start some of the first libraries in America because he knew reading and learning were so important.

After working for other printers for many years, Ben started his own printing shop. He wrote about his own ideas and used parts of the paper to talk about good morals. Morals are the things that are good to do in life -- like being honest, being kind, not stealing and working hard. Ben made lists of what he wanted to do better each day then at the end of the day checked the boxes on what he did good at and made note of what he needed to do better. He believed improving each day was very important.

Ben was very interested in science and invention. He studied electricity. At the time no one had electricity, which means they had no lights or electronics like we do today. Ben saw lightning during a storm and guessed that it must be electricity. Sometimes when lightning hit tall buildings it started fires. Ben had the idea to put a metal pole on the top of buildings, so when the lightning struck the pole it would go into the ground instead of start fires. This invention was called a lightning rod. Many people think that Ben used a kite to discover lightning was electricity, but he really just wrote about the idea and someone else tried it.

Ben also invented a certain type of eye glasses called bifocals, which allowed someone to see differently depending on the part of the glasses they were looking through. Ben also liked to play chess. He also created the first Fire Department and helped start some of the first universities in the United States.

Because of his newspapers and his inventions and other achievements Ben Franklin became very well known in America and across the ocean in Europe. When many Americans disagreed with England about taxes, Ben was on the side of the Americans who wanted change. He wrote about his ideas and even helped Thomas Jefferson write the Declaration of Independence. The Declaration of Independence was a paper they wrote to tell England they wanted to be their own country and to be free.

A war began between America and England, so Ben took a ship across the ocean to ask for France's help. The French people loved Ben Franklin. He liked to wear a fur hat and talk about science and his inventions. They thought he was interesting and fun to talk to. France ended up helping America fight and later win the war against England.

In his new country, Ben helped put together the first Constitution. The Constitution was a list of laws to help the country stay together and work well. To the end of his life Ben did all he could to help make America a strong country.

Earlier we talked about some of the morals, good things we should do, that Ben wrote about in his paper. Ben wasn't a perfect person, like all of us, but he wanted to do good things.

He wrote about temperance. **Temperance** is not doing too much of something such as eating. We need good food for our bodies, but too much of it isn't always a good thing. We can usually tell by how our stomachs feel when we are eating.

He also taught about **silence**. Sometimes it's good to speak up, but other times it's better to listen and think about what we should say. If we don't think before we speak, we often say things we don't really mean.

Order means to think about what we are doing and have a plan. We shouldn't spend all our time doing the same thing, but giving the right amount of time to each good thing.

Frugality means to be careful with the money that you have. It's easy to want to spend all of your money, but it's better to spend money on what you need and to save some. It's ok to spend some of your money on fun things, but not all of it.

Industry means to stay busy doing useful things. Each day we can make a plan of what we want to do and then get to work. Having fun is good in its own time, but we should also spend time learning, helping others, and getting chores and other things done.

Justice means treating others well and doing our best to make things fair.

Cleanliness means we should take care of our bodies by keeping them cleaning, bathing each day, and brushing our teeth.

Like Ben, we can do our best to live by these teachings each day. You could even keep track of your goals like Ben did in his journals and checklists. You can also read and learn and come up with new ideas that will help other people like Ben's lightning rod. You can also be courageous and stand up for good things like Ben did during the Revolution.

"Buffalo Bill" Cody

Greatest Showman of the West

Close your eyes and imagine you live in America in the 1800s, a time before cars, the Internet and TV. You are riding in a wagon pulled by your family's best two horses. Your mom and dad are up front and you and your siblings are in the back. You look around and see many other families also riding towards the main event. When the wagon stops you climb out and hurry to a stand where your father buys tickets and hands you one. You give your ticket to attendant then rush into the large arena and climb up the stairs to what you think is the best seat with the best view. You smell popcorn and your mother hands you a bag with a smile. You take a bite and wait in anticipation for the show to begin.

Suddenly a gun fires and you hear the thunder of hooves as a stampede of horses fill the arena. Dust clouds fill the air. Indians whoop and holler. Army men shoot their guns and flash their swords. Soon a battle begins. But this isn't a real battle, it's just a show, and the crowd watches in amazement as the showmen act out a battle from American history. An soldier cries out and falls off his horses. An Indian charges and waves his tomahawk. The smell of gunpowder fills the air. Soon the dust and the smoke settles. The battle is finished. The audience cheers wildly.

Suddenly a lone man rides into the arena, waving his hat. From his leather coat, long hair and mustache, you instantly recognize the rider as the greatest showman of the Wild West -- Buffalo Bill Cody. You wave your hat and cheer too. The show has just begun and you can't wait to see what comes next.

Bill Cody was born in 1847 on a farm outside Le Claire, Iowa to Isaac and Mary Ann Cody. When Bill was young slavery was still happening in some parts of the country. Bill's father, Isaac, was very much against it. Many people didn't like Bill's family for this reason. One day when his father was speaking out against slavery someone hurt him very badly. After this Isaac had to move away to avoid his enemies. Later, the same group planned to catch Isaac and hurt him again. When Bill heard what they were going to do to his father, he jumped on his horse and rode 30 miles to warn him before they came.

Not long afterward Bill's father became very sick and soon passed away. This left Bill to help take care of his family when he was only 11 years old. His first job was with a wagon company. He rode his horse up and down the train of wagons and delivered messages to help them keep in touch with each other.

When Bill was 14 years old gold was discovered in California and many Americans hurried there in hopes to mine gold and become rich. This was called a Gold Rush. Bill left on his horse for California, but along the way he found a job delivering mail from one place to another. Because there were no telephones, mail by horse was the only way people could talk to each other.

A few years later, Bill joined the Army's 3rd Cavalry, which was fighting the Native Indians in what was called the Plains Wars. Bill was the Chief of the Scouts. His job was to ride ahead and see if they were going to be attacked. He fought in sixteen battles with the army.

While the army was on the trail they needed food, so one of Bill's jobs was to hunt buffalo. Buffalo are huge, wild, hairy animals with horns that roamed the plains during the Wild West. At this time there were hundreds and thousands of buffalo and Bill became a very skilled hunter of them.

Once, another hunter with the same name as Bill challenged him to see who could hunt the most buffalo within 8 hours. Whoever won would keep the name "Buffalo Bill." The race was on. Bill took off on his horse and raced around the massive herd of buffalo, aiming his long rifle, and firing, picking them off one at a time. He kicked his horse faster and faster, aiming and firing, aiming and firing, buffalos dropping at every shot. When the time was up, someone rode around and counted the buffalo. Bill had killed more beasts than the other man and won the name "Buffalo Bill."

Often people came from the East Coast or other parts of the world to visit the Wild West and hunt the famous buffalo. Buffalo Bill started taking these visitors on trips to explore the West and hunt. Some of the people who went with Bill wrote about him in the newspapers and someone even made him a character in a book. Soon many people knew about this famous hunter of the American West.

A few years later Buffalo Bill joined a traveling show called The Scouts of the Prairie. Together with the other actors he would act out famous battles for audiences. These shows were very popular and often they performed to sold out crowds. Everyone was excited to see the famous Buffalo Bill Cody and gun fighters such as "Wild Bill" Hickok.

Before long, Bill had the idea to start his own show and called it Buffalo Bill's Wild West. He and his crew dressed in colorful costumes and acted out battles with guns and horses while a live band played music. Many of the acts included horses and their riders from all across the world from Spanish Cowboys to Turks, Arabs, and Mongols from Asia. The American Indian war hero Sitting Bull was in the show along with famous women sharp shooters such as Annie Oakley and Calamity Jane. People came from all across the country to be entertained by Buffalo Bill and his talented performers.

Later Buffalo Bill's West West show took a ship across the ocean to Europe, where they performed before such royalty as the Queen of England and the Kings of France and Germany. They also performed nearby the Chicago's Worlds Fair and were a huge hit.

Buffalo Bill used the money from his world famous show to found his own town in Wyoming and called it Cody. There he bought land and built a beautiful hotel and brought in cattle for a very large ranch. He designed Cody so people from all over could visit the countryside and pretend to be cowboys, go on horseback rides, and hunt animals in the woods. These activities were some of his great loves and he wanted to share them with others.

Even though Bill fought against Indians early in his life, he later had great respect for them and their simple way of life. He knew the reason many of them attacked settlers was because they had been treated poorly in the first place. He felt bad for what had been done to them, that they had been driven from their lands by the new

Americans. He believed they should be treated with respect and hired many of them to work for his show and paid the same as everyone else.

Bill spent much of his time in nature, so he came to have great respect for the land and animals of the American West. He later did what he could to help preserve these beautiful places. This is called conservationism. Americans like he and Teddy Roosevelt believed that much of the land should be kept safe, so it can be enjoyed by everyone. This is why we have National Parks today.

Spend some time thinking about what it would have been like to start taking care of your family like Bill did at a young age. It was hard and probably scary at times, but Bill learned new skills such as hunting and horseback riding. When you face challenges remember that sticking with things until you get better is the only way to learn and grow. So be sure to face hard things with courage and keep on trying.

Like Buffalo Bill you can use your imagination to come up with new ideas to entertain others. Spend some time thinking of an act or show you could perform and share it with a family member or a friend. If you can make someone else smile or laugh, that is a very good thing.

Also, spend a little more time outside. There is much to appreciate outdoors, even if it is your backyard. Take the time to look at the sky and clouds and the trees and the listen to the birds in them. There is much to be enjoyed in the natural world around you if you take the time to notice it.

J.K. Rowling

The Harry Potter Story

Do you remember the last time you were playing and you got so lost in your imagination that it felt like real life? That is always an amazing experience and often kids experience it a lot more than adults. I think adults could learn a few things from kids about what real imagination and play is like, don't you?

Inside your brain are very small things called neurons which help create your thoughts and memories and imagination. Did you know there are more neurons in your brain than stars in the galaxy? That is one of the many things that makes you an amazing being. Just think of the incredible things you can dream up and imagine and do with that awesome power alone.

One such child like you was a girl named Joanne Rowling, but her friends and family called her "Jo." Jo lived in England with her mom and dad and younger sister named Dianne. Like you, Jo had a big imagination and loved playing in the woods and dreaming up magical stories. She wrote her first book at age six and called it "Rabbit." After she wrote these stories she would read them to her little sister. Jo was also very close to her mother who often read to her at night.

When Jo was in primary school she was pretty normal at most subjects, but was especially good at English and writing. Around this time, her mother became sick with a disease called multiple sclerosis. This made it hard for her to do things like walk and move her body. This wasn't easy for Jo, because she loved her mom and was very close to her. Her mother had always encouraged her to keep writing and doing what she loved most.

After primary school Jo wanted to go to one of the best colleges in England called Oxford. She was sad when she found out they wouldn't let her in, so she went to a different college called Exeter where she studied French and the Classics. She did well enough in college, but her favorite past time was to read books by great authors such as Charles Dickens and JRR Tolkien, who wrote The Lord of the Rings and The Hobbit. Jo wanted to write her own book someday, but was still waiting for her big idea to come.

After college, Jo got a job and one day she was on a very long train ride from Manchester to London. During the ride she suddenly imagined a little boy on the train going far away to a school for wizards. A picture of this boy began to form in her mind -- he had brown hair, glasses and a scar on his forehead. After the train ride she hurried home as fast as he could and began writing her story. She named the boy Harry Potter and began to dream up his adventures at the school for wizards. Finally, Jo's big idea had come and more than anything she wanted to share her big idea with others! She planned to write seven different books about Harry Potter and his magical world.

Around this time Jo's mother passed away from multiple sclerosis. It was a very hard time for Jo and she took all of her sad feelings and used many of them in her story about Harry Potter, who also lost his parents and spent much time wanting to be with them again. Sometimes when people are sad, they write to help them work through their feelings.

While Jo was writing, she saw an ad in the newspaper for a job in Portugal teaching English. She thought it sounded interesting to go somewhere new, so she packed up her things and took a plane to this new country. While in Portugal she would work on her story during the day and teach English at night. She met a journalist while living there and they got married and had a baby who she named Jessica after one of her favorite authors. In Portugal Jo and her husband struggled with their marriage and eventually it got so bad that she moved to Scotland with her baby. In Scotland she didn't have a job, because she spent all of her time taking care of her baby Jessica.

During the day Jo would take Jessica on walks around the city until she fell asleep. Once Jessica was asleep, Jo would go to cafes and sit and write her story. Because real life was so hard for Jo, she found that writing about the magical life of Harry Potter made her happy for a time.

Eventually Jo's first book was finished and she called it Harry Potter and the Philosopher's Stone. In the book after Harry leaves his horrible relatives, the Dursley's, and takes a train to the Hogwarts School of Witchcraft and Wizardry, he becomes friends with two other students, Ron Weasley and Hermione Granger. Together they learn about the mysteries of the school, deal with bullies, play a magical game called Quidditch, and come face to face with

Lord Voldemort, the world's most evil wizard who wants nothing more than to stop Harry and his friends.

Next Jo started looking for an agent, someone who would help her publish the book. A publisher is a company who prints and makes copies of the books and sends them to stores to be sold. No one knew who Jo was, so it was a while before anyone would even read her book. At least 12 publishers sent letters saying they weren't interested in Harry Potter. Jo was frustrated but kept trying.

Finally, the head of one publisher took Jo's first chapter home and instead of reading it himself gave it to his 8 year old daughter, Alice. Alice read the first chapter and loved it. She said it was better than anything else she had read. She wanted the second chapter immediately! Her father and the publishing company Bloomsbury decided to publish Harry Potter and Jo would use the pen name JK Rowling! Jo was so excited!

Before long, Harry Potter and the Sorcerer's Stone became very popular in England. It began to win awards and eventually won book of the year there. Jo's dreams were coming true. She began to work on the next book and soon an American publisher, Scholastic, bought the rights to her book for $100,000. This was the most that had ever been offered for a children's book. Harry Potter was a major hit!

Parents and teachers across the world were excited to see young children reading such large books at a time when many were worried that kids were watching too much TV instead.

Soon the Harry Potter books became movies and Jo wrote more books. At times it was hard for her to keep writing and coming up with new ideas and creating stories that worked. Sometimes she would take breaks to get her creativity back. Creativity and imagination can't always be forced. But finally Joe finished the seventh and final book, Harry Potter and the Deathly Hallows, the series was finished!

From all of the books and movies and other Harry Potter merchandise sold, Joanne Rowling became the richest woman in England -- and a billionaire. But Jo remembered how hard it was when she was poor and a single mom trying to take care of her baby. She remembered how hard it was for her mom when she suffered from multiple sclerosis. So Jo spent much of her time thinking about how she could give back to others less fortunate than herself. She began giving much of her money away to charities, many of which helped single moms and children and those who had multiple sclerosis.

Because Joanne gave so much away she isn't a billionaire anymore -- but she doesn't care. She knows that using her money to help others makes her more happy than having a lot of money. She knows you don't need to be rich to be happy. True happiness comes from giving to others and seeing the smile on the face of someone who has enjoyed her books about Harry Potter.

Take some time to think about what you enjoy doing, the things that make you the happiest and cause you to use your imagination and get lost in what you are doing. Think of what you might do to get a little better at those skills. Maybe it means drawing or writing or practicing a sport or learning how to solve a math problem better. It might be playing the piano or another instrument. Remember, you have a mind as wide and as beautiful as the galaxy and can do incredible things when you put your heart and mind and time to it.

The Pony Express

Brave Riders of the American West

Can you imagine living in a time when were no cell phones, no email and no other electronic way to talk to others living far away? For a very long time that is how everyone lived. Instead of making phone calls they wrote letters, and often it took many days for them to arrive. Imagine if you had something very important to tell someone, but they wouldn't find out until weeks later!

In the United States, during the the 1800s, the days of pioneers and cowboys, there lived a creative business man named William Russell. William Russell had a genius idea. He thought of a way to send letters across the country very fast. To do this he used horses and riders who rode as fast as they could from one stop to another. From the state of Missouri to California, across thousands of miles they built many stations. At each station a new horse and a new rider waited. There, as a soon as a rider arrived, the new rider grabbed the mail and rode as fast as they could to the next station. Instead of letters taking a very long time, they moved across the country is just 10 days. That was very fast! Russell called his new company The Pony Express.

Russells riders need to be fast and also very brave. The journey from Missouri to California was often very dangerous. They could be attacked by wild animals or bandits who wanted to take the mail. The posters looking for riders said: "Young, skinny, wiry fellows, not over 18. Must be expert riders. Willing to risk death daily. Orphans preferred." Even though the job was dangerous, many brave, young riders volunteered to help.

One of these riders was Bill Cody. Bill was only 15 at the time he started riding for The Pony Express. During one of his trips from Wyoming, he was riding his horse when suddenly an entire gang of Indians burst out of the trees and started chasing him on their horses. Bill looked back in fear as they raised their guns and started firing at him. Bullets whizzed past his head, as he ducked and spurred the horse as hard as he could. The horse moved faster and faster as the natives fired again and again. Bill thought for sure he was done for, but he cried out to the horse and kicked and rode faster, lying flat against the horse's back. Soon, the natives disappeared behind him and he rode and rode until reaching the next station. Later Bill picked up the nickname "Buffalo" Bill Cody and became famous for his show that toured all across America.

Another famous Pony Express ride was Bob Haslam, who became known as "Pony" Bob. Bob was born in England and came across the ocean to America when he was just a boy. His family moved to Salt Lake City and there he worked on a ranch and as a messenger. He was known for being brave and loyal and always got the job done. Loyal is when someone can trust you because you always do what you say you are going to do.

When Bob was 20 he joined the Pony Express. Like Bill Cody, he rode at a time when Native Americans were very dangerous in the area. During one ride he got to the station only to find that Indians were on the warpath and he could not stop. So even though he and his horse were very tired he kept on riding. Bob persevered. Perseverance is when you keep doing something even though you are tired and want to give up. Bob kept riding until he reached the next station, only to find that it was under attack as well! Bob did not know what to do. He and his horse were tired and hungry. He knew he had to get the job done and deliver the mail, so he continued riding! Once he reached the next station he handed his mail off and rested for 9 hours. But Bob wasn't done yet. He picked up the next bag of mail, hopped on his horse, and rode back the other direction. His 380-mile trip was the longest Pony Express ride in history. From then on he was known as "Pony" Bob and remembered for his amazing ride.

Later, when Pony Bob grew old and passed away the newspaper printed "'Pony Bob' Haslam, Who Knew No Fear, Dies in Chicago -- a man once famous throughout the United States for his courage, endurance and skill."

Although the Pony Express was an amazing venture, it only lasted a year and a half. The telegraph was invented a few years later. The telegraph was very long wire that its designers stretched all the way across the country. The wire was used to send messages across it at lightning speeds. Because of this the Pony Express was no longer needed. But riders like “Pony” Bob, “Buffalo” Bill, and others will always be remembered for their strength, bravery and perseverance.

First Transcontinental Railroad
Engineering Miracle of the American West

All across the world trains are extremely important, because they move goods and people from one place to another and can do it very quickly. Railroads are one of the most important parts of American History, because the country is very big and they helped connect the East and the West.

Many years ago it took a very long time to travel from the East to the West. Most people had to take a boat all the way around the continent, a journey which took months to complete. Travellers could also take a wagon across the dangerous wilderness and tall mountains to get from one side of the country to another. Either way, it was a very difficult journey and kept the country separated in many ways.

But in the 1800s gold was discovered in the West and many Americans moved there to try and strike it rich. But one major problem was how long it took to get to the gold. One man, Asa Whitney, believed a railroad could be built right through the the middle of the country. Many doubted this could be done, but Asa made a plan and went to the government with his idea, but at first no progress was made.

Later, an American named Theodore Judah decided to find a way to build a railroad across the country. He was a surveyor. A surveyor is someone who looks at the land with special tools and finds ways to build roads and buildings on it. Theodore had many good ideas about how the railroad could be built. He had to learn much about math and other sciences in order to design maps that could be used to make a path for the railroad.

Eventually two big companies, the Union Pacific Railroad and the Central Pacific Railroad caught the vision of the railroad and decided to make it happen. They would call it the Transcontinental Railroad. Soon afterward one company started in California and the other started in Nebraska with a plan to meet in the middle.

Building the railroad across the United Stated was a dangerous task and extremely difficult at times. They had to build tall bridges across wide rivers. To go through mountains they had to dig deep holes, then place gun powder in them and blow them up to create even deeper holes that went all the way through the mountain. Many smart engineers worked on creating a path for the 2000 miles of track that were being laid.

Railroad tracks were laid by pounding spikes into railroad ties. All of this work was done by hand, by pounding each spike in with a hammer. This was very difficult work and many workers didn't survive the hard labor. Americans of all different races and colors helped build the railroad. One group that did much of the work were Chinese immigrants. An immigrant is someone who comes from another country. Chinese immigrants worked long and hard for very little pay to help complete the monumental task.

In 1869 after eight years of work the two companies met in the middle at Promontory Point, Utah. They threw a big party to celebrate the completion of the railroad. A gold spike had been prepared as the last spike in the railroad. President of the Central Pacific Railroad, Governor Stanford gave a speech then lifted a hammer to pound the last spike into the ground. But he swung and missed! The crowd burst out laughing. "He missed it!" They said. He swung again and hit the gold spike in. Everyone cheered!

News of the finished railroad was sent by telegram to both parts of the country. When it reached New York and California they fired off cannons to show their excitement. It was truly an exciting time for the United States of America! A trip across the country that had taken many months now only took 10 days! The new Transcontinental Railroad was truly an engineer miracle of hard work and smart minds all working together to accomplish a common task.

Sandra Porter

My Grandmother

Sometimes we think heroes always have to be someone who makes the history books or the news. But often great things happen in smaller ways. Heroes can be the people you are around every day, like your mom and dad, or a teacher or someone who is just going to work everyday. The world works because many people are doing small things in their own little corner of the world. This story is about a hero the author knows personally, his grandmother, who did great things for her family and those around her.

Sandra was born in the small southern Utah town of Escalante on the 4th of July. Whenever her birthday came around and there were fireworks she thought the fireworks were to celebrate her birthday. And because of her personality Sandra was often referred to as a "firecracker" herself.

Bedtime History

Sandra's father was a rancher and her mother was a busy home maker who excelled at every aspect of home management. Together they lived on the outskirts of town with a big barn, fruit trees, a pig pen, chicken coup and big ditch, that made for fun, endless playtime. Music was an important part of Sandra's childhood. She practiced and practiced until she was very good. Then as a teenager she played the organ and directed music at church.

Sandra's family owned the local movie theater and she was the popcorn girl and had to sweep up after every show, a job which she strongly disliked.

When Sandra grew up she met a handsome young man named Bob. She loved his flashy car and cute sense of humor. They sent letters back and forth for two years, while Bob was in the army. After Sandra graduated from high school, she and Bob went to college for a while, and then they were married in 1955. Their first daughter, Melanie, was born in 1956, but sadly passed away three days later. Sandra was very sad, but was fortunate to have loving family and friends who supported her through this hard time. One year later another baby girl was born but passed away prematurely. These were tough years for Sandra, because she wanted so much to be a mother.

After Bob graduated from college with a degree in education, they moved to Mesa, Arizona. Sandra thought only crazy people would live in such a hot place as Arizona.

A few years later their next daughter, Teresa, was born, then they had a baby boy and named him Brent. Sandra was so excited to finally be a mother and loved doing it. During these years they purchased a piano and Sandra began teaching piano lessons and piano theory. Over the last 45 years she has taught many young people and some of her students went on to become very talented, well-known pianists.

Later they adopted a baby boy named Travis and Sandra was so excited to be a mother again.

With her talents in music, Sandra has also composed many of her own songs for her family. Eventually her children had their own children and her life has been blessed by many beautiful grandchildren, who love her very much for her kindness and spunk. Every year on the 4th of July and her birthday they love watching Sandra jump into the pool with all of her clothes on! It has become a fun, yearly tradition.

Sandra's life hasn't always been easy, but it has been filled with friends and family and many beautiful moments marked by her love and zest for life.

Made in the USA
Monee, IL
14 December 2019

18579054R00065